And so to Bard

Robin Charlton

BookLeaf Publishing

Presentation by *BookLeaf Publishing*

Web: www.bookleafpub.com

E-mail: info@bookleafpub.com

ISBN: 9789357211444

First edition 2022

DEDICATION

To everything that breathes in.......and wonders how!

ACKNOWLEDGEMENT

To all my friends, family and The Trio. I'm so glad I met you all.

PREFACE

A picture is worth a thousand words and a poem is worth a thousand feelings.

The Will To Live

In the morning and when I rise,
I wipe the sleep from my eyes,
And listen, listen to what's inside
The message from my inner lives,
I will stand ready, willing and seeking to serve
To give of my life to that which deserves,
Sometimes it's quiet and hard to find,
As if it's best days we're far behind,
There's a longing to make a difference here,
My purpose revealing, becoming more clear,
And if it's warm and I can give
And connect, in part to The Will To Live,
Let it be graced with the ease to forgive
Under the mantle of Live and Let Live
For there is in me a deep deep cry
To be of some account before I die.

In quiet moments

Inner stillness, that's the key
To appreciate thy wondrous majesty
Spinning spheres of eternity
Blending with ethereal symmetry
The human and creation in harmony
With quietness and serenity
Could we find our destiny
Through such softness and tranquility?
To my essence and to me, how fortunate are we.

EVERY DAY

Everyday,
In a remedial way, to give myself a clean slate,

Everyday,
In a thankful way, to have gratitude for all that
I've been given,

Everyday,
In a warm hearted way, to remember to smile,

Everyday,
In an unselfish way, to give something away,

Everyday
In a refreshing way, to keep myself clean,

Everyday
In a self chosen way, to arrange myself to
receive,

Everyday
In a constant way, to practice being open.

In the greenhouse

Some seeds were planted in a tray,
I watered them and went away,
some days pass and can there be
any green shoots for me to see?
Nothing, I leave, a little downhearted,
But the next day I look and it's just started
But wait, They're so small, there's a doubt
No, it's fine, tiny shoots are poking out
I sigh with relief and exasperation
In witness to this regeneration
Now, they quicken each day a little bigger
But how is if caused, What pulls thc trigger?
What causes these seedlings to grow?
I really would like to know
Supernatural. Or Mythical
It certainly is a miracle!

A Fresh Start

Like the freshness of Spring arrives and more
light rushes in
New start hope, a chance to be new, again, to
begin
To make a new start if that's your aim,
Perhaps you could begin by changing your name
For it's easy to be fixed in old fashioned ways
Arrested, bogged down in well trodden paths
Come at it fresh, come at it new
Add something new to all that you do
Change the rhythm, open the door
It's not like it was, it's different from before
Make lots of small efforts to rearrange
Let's resist the urge to make a big change
For let's not be forgetting,
That there's a new epoch onsetting
A new start hope could be the vitamin
That occupies us during the interim.

Wonders Guide Me

Life is a many splendored thing,
For we can laugh, cry or sing
In an Aladdin's cave of so much given
Enlivened by a purpose driven,
And so with reverence to this rarity
To develop a life of quality
Radiate this richness to others
Spread the bounty to sisters and brothers
Make a mark to be of some account
No barriers here, I can't surmount
This life can be a sacred dance
Making the most of this enhanced chance
Agents for God are you and me
Gently now, let it go free

A New Epoch

Blow on the Trumpets
Clap your hands
Call all the Singers
Strike up the Bands
Summon us all to bring our best
Working for God, we never rest
Push back the space for those yet to come,
Light all the Lamps, the stars and the Sun
Carry the torch of burning desire
Light up the darkness with our living fire
Bring on the future, let's be it's friend
On us, the unseen may depend
Time turns over a brand new page
A new epoch of a silver age.

A mark against Judgement

It doesn't matter if you're big or small,
It really doesn't matter at all,
Who cares if your skin is white or brown
Or if you're a Jew, or if you're a Clown,
No one cares if you can't spell, or if you've got
no gold to sell,
It doesn't matter if you're Young or Old
Or it doesn't match up to what you've been told
And will you care what they say when your time
is done
Will there be a tally of a race well run
Be kind to yourself and to one another
Realise all are sister and brother
For when you judge, you strike with a rod
Another like you, another piece of God
It heats you up when you bear a grudge
So, live and let live and don't be a judge
Try to be still and feel inside
The spirit within you that resides.

A Ponder

Today I saw a Passion flower with a Bee
That felt so wonderful to me
For, in this culture, cruel with little pardon
So far removed from this Emerald garden
This kind, warm grace that passes here
Anaesthetises pain and banishes fear
Charges the Aura, now full and clean
With a force most gentle, some known and seen
Noise and worry start to cease
My soul is settled and at peace
Shine on then, with Emerald power
Servicing all, hour by hour
Radiating goodness and hope for tomorrow
Lifting me away from doubt and sorrow.
Thank you Mother Nature for all you do
I am so proud to be a part of you.

TRUST

Trust is a securing embrace
A reassuring, confirming grace
A confidence shared
From a position declared
Trust eradicates doubt and leaves nothing liable
There's no need to swear on the Bible
Trust is a lance that banishes suspicion
Grants no space for criticism.

Trust is seen with a Blind man and his dog,
Trust can elevate us out of the fog,
It's with the mother duck and her young
And with a baby whose life has just begun,
And when we go to bed at night,
We trust, with eyes closed, we'll be all right
And when we rise to another new day
Let's trust in good things to light our way.

Opal moments

Tune in, firstly, to yourself,
For there is inside, an extraordinary wealth
Of wisdom, experience and questions
Reheats, memories and suggestions,
Codings, feelings and considerations
Meditations, prayers and deliberations
A supermarket of glowing gems
Refreshing me as they cleanse
Tune in then, to your cavern,
Let Opal take you to Mars or Saturn
Or to a tree or to a flower
Unlimited is our personal power
We are known by the words we speak
And by the fact, that each life is unique
They say 'what we think is what we become'
Take note then, of what you've done

A message to the Human Race

Another message to the human race
Listen to hear this sacred grace
There's a chance to build something fine
Between the high and the low, a vine
With devotion, try and some resistance
To make a clean return with one's existence
On a planet made coarse by those who don't
care
That dulls and lessens the humans flair
Let us light beacons out into the night
So that the darkness may be filled with light
For could it be that we few,in time
Become God's agents within the vine.

May the children have clean air to breathe
May, so called leaders, - nor deceive
Or pretend that they're not corrupt
When all that does is disrupt
Let the Ladies hold their heads up high
No longer should they have to cry
Or be wary of every passer by
So let the wonders never cease
Pray that in the future, they'll be more peace
For we all have a soul and spirit within
Perhaps, one day, mankind will be of kin

Significance

The human machine is a magnificence
And as we search for it's significance
Remember we're born in the image of creation
To break our own stop situation
Desperation must make some try
To arrange their like to attract the high
For me, this life is just the start
A melody between head and heart
And as I go about my days
I'll practice the arts of creations ways
It may seen a little strange,
That to receive, I must arrange
So, to realign and make a change
God and the human, in interchange.

Another day

Let's be thankful for another day
Another chance to strengthen our way
Today, all was there before me
The clouds, trees, birds and bees
We're already busy about the day
I witnessed this and was caused to be still
And to appreciate the rising thrill of joy from deep within,
That this day, this moment, was new
It looked the same, but that wasn't true
This day is unique and I am passing through
I am getting old, but I've just begun
To sing the songs I should have done, when I was young

An Opal moment

The man suddenly pointed to a spot on the hill
Where he thought he saw something, but now it was still
What caught his eye was a shepherd, guiding his flock
He's governed not by agenda or a ticking clock
A solitary union, alone but busy
Not to be witnessed in a town or a city
For the mountain air is fresh
There's little pollution,
The shepherd is with his daily communion
The Opal, then a sanctuary
Where the host can fill the vacancy
Perhaps, the only clean space the higher can find,
Is in our Opal state of mind

Seeking a way to serve

Born empty but in God's image
Granted a faculty truly devine
Blessed with a life, a soul and a spirit,
Charged to connect with the blooded vine

Gifted an amazing can-do machine
To keep the wonder of creation clean
With mind alert and senses keen
A sacred dance with the unseen

This is how to refine and do
While we're here on this planet blue
The host persuades us how to be
To let our soul and spirit free

So I pray with this quiet voice
To make well the supreme gift of choice
For I've been given more than I deserve
I must find a true way to serve.

The Faithful one

When, at times I don't believe,
Or find somehow I've been deceived,
When untruth stings with sharp deception,
Irritated by another misconception
When I see the desperation
In the eyes of every nation,
Should I cry? Or should I try?

Even when I don't really care,
I know, I know it's always there
It waits for me, it always has done
Since my journey first begun
I make many returns
To find that the fire still burns
To be within and it with me

To tune in, to be the same
And to do it in God's name
It feels like coming home
And with my kind, I'm not alone
A simple man, I want to be,
Doing God's work, unreservedly.

Under a Tree on Hampstead Heath

Sometimes I wish I could have been there,
Would I have stopped, would I have stared?
To see a young boy sitting under a tree?
Would I know how profound this act could be
Every Saturday, come rain or shine,
From early morning, until supper time
Under a tree on Hampstead Heath
A young boy sat underneath
Petitioning the God's to show him the truth
This was no misspent youth
An innocent act, so decent and clean
Could he have grasped what that would mean?
Who could have known what was to be
Because a boy sat under a tree?

.

ON THE STEPS

Mighty matters are at hand
To huge to really understand
Some know and ache for change
For misaligned humans to rearrange,
Once, a few met, to answer a call
On the steps of Peterborough Town Hall,
Against. All the odds, they took a stance
To give something unseen a chance.

Each week, they meet to take a position
To let the God's know of their petition
They gather quietly, but with insistence
That they're endeavours could make a difference

Perhaps their meetings, year after year,
Constitute a passion of things quiet dear
Their constant efforts in the same direction
Never minding about perfection.

So, if you're passing the Town Hall,
Or wondering 'What there is to do at all?
The passion starts at half past eight
Every Tuesday, it's a date.

When you join us, you will feel

That this attempt is very real
We'll never be in any doubt
That the fire we lit will never go out.
It stands as a beacon for all that's right
To guide all searchers towards the light.

THE FLUTE PLAYER

A man played his flute in Leicester Square
He played it as if no one was there,
That moment his playing was in communion
A simple tune was his union
To surrender for a while, to be out of the way,
For choirs of the host to come out to play
It's as if there's no price or cost
To find ways to be hopelessly lost
Elevated, uplifted, like a spirit flare
With no concern for whoever is there,
So if you get lost in what you love to do,
Then perhaps, this phenomena may happen to
you.

Even more determined

Why am I surrounded by so many lies
Why do you hide behind your disguise?
Do you think we are fools and not very wise?
That we will endorse your evil enterprise?

Your entities of bitter persuasion
Tarnish the majesty of every nation
Have we all gone completely insane?
What will it win? What will it gain?

For when we hear the screams of pain
As your bombs unleash their deadly strain,
I WILL TURN AWAY, away again
To champion a better way
For we can be a beacon for the Devine
Strengthen the tendrils of the Gemin Vine
Keep the best of human kind
Clean essences for you to find
It's time now to build a Temple of love
To be filled with angels from above
To be 'one of them' over there
One of them that really cares.

www.ingramcontent.com/pod-product-compliance
Lightning Source LLC
Chambersburg PA
CBHW051756130826
49812CB00033B/1176
9789357211444